TRACING

SCOTTISH ANCESTORS

Simon Fowler

D0928863

PUBLIC RECORD OFFICE

Public Record Office
Richmond
Surrey
TW9 4DU

ISBN 1 903365 02 3

A catalogue card for this book
is available from the British Library

085711962

PPR

Front cover: William Brand Esq. of Glasgow
Photograph by John Scott Alexander of Glasgow
Registered for copyright by
Alexander Bros. of Glasgow 5 May 1892
(COPY I/408)

Printed by Cromwell Press, Trowbridge, Wiltshire

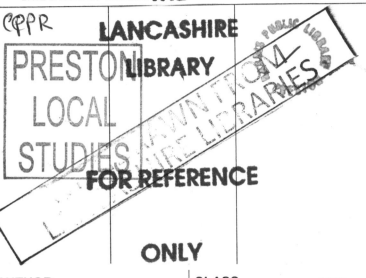

AUTHOR	CLASS	GI PPR
FOWLER, S.		929.1FOW

TITLE

Tracing Scottish ancestors

Public Record Office
Pocket Guides to Family History

Getting Started in Family History

Using Birth, Marriage and Death Records

Using Census Returns

Using Wills

Using Army Records

Using Navy Records

Tracing Irish Ancestors

Tracing Scottish Ancestors

Using Poor Law Records

Tracing Catholic Ancestors

Tracing Nonconformist Ancestors

CONTENTS

INTRODUCTION	7
HISTORICAL BACKGROUND	8
The administration of Scotland	9
GENERAL REGISTER OFFICE FOR SCOTLAND	11
Introduction	11
– Charges for access	12
Scots Origins	12
Statutory registers of births, marriages and deaths	13
Census returns	17
Old parish registers	19
Other records at New Register House	21
NATIONAL ARCHIVES OF SCOTLAND	22
Nonconformist registers	25
Testaments and inventories	25
– Testament tips	27
Retours or services of heirs	28
Sasines	28
Kirk Session records	29
FAMILY RECORDS CENTRE	30
Birth, marriage and death records after 1 July 1837	31
– Scot Link	31

– Armed forces returns	32
Census returns	33
Nonconformist registers	34
Wills	35
PUBLIC RECORD OFFICE	36
Military records	38
Army	41
– Officers	41
– Other ranks	42
Royal Air Force and Royal Navy	43
Merchant seamen	45
Emigration	47
– Further reading	49
The Hudson's Bay Company	50
Immigration	51
Some other sources	52
– Minor sources	53
SPECIALIST LIBRARIES	54
Society of Genealogists	54
Scottish Genealogy Society	58
OTHER RESOURCES	60
GLOSSARY	61
FURTHER READING	62

INTRODUCTION

This *Pocket Guide* offers a brief introduction to finding out more about your Scottish ancestors. In many ways hunting for these people is easier than tracing English forebears. The collections of the General Register Office for Scotland at New Register House are simpler to use, and more informative, than their English equivalents; and fortunately an increasing amount of research can be conducted over the internet.

In England, you can trace Scottish ancestors through the main centres for family history – the Public Record Office (PRO), the Family Records Centre (FRC) and the Society of Genealogists (SoG), all in London. Relevant records at the PRO were largely created because of the involvement of Scots in services, such as the armed forces and the Coastguard, that were administered centrally from Westminster. The FRC's material about Scots who lived south of the border includes census returns and Prerogative Court of Canterbury wills, while the Society of Genealogists' library holds much about Scotland and the Scottish, as well as microfilm copies of documents that are normally only available in Edinburgh.

When researching Scottish ancestors it is important to remember that Scotland has separate legal and administrative traditions from England and Wales, although it has been part of the United Kingdom for nearly 300 years. The Act of Union of 1707 guaranteed the independence of the Scottish church, the legal system, and education. These guarantees – and the very different nature of Scottish society – have been jealously guarded, and have affected the way in which records have been created, preserved and made available to researchers.

HISTORICAL BACKGROUND

In order to trace Scottish ancestors it is important to understand something of the country's history and constitution. For this has influenced not just where the records are kept, but how they were created and preserved in the first place.

Until 1707 Scotland was a separate and independent kingdom within the British Isles. When Elizabeth I died in 1603, her cousin James VI of Scotland ascended the throne of England and became James I. Despite the unifying presence of a common monarch, the two kingdoms remained very different; indeed, there was even a short war in 1639–40. It was perhaps inevitable, however, that formal union would eventually follow: economic and social factors were driving the two peoples closer together.

When the Act of Union was passed in 1707, it was very much a union of policy, as the novelist and journalist Daniel Defoe called it, not a union of affection. What motivated the politicians was the fear that, on the death of childless Queen Anne, the Scots might choose a Catholic king, James Edward Stuart, rather than a Protestant monarch, George, Elector of Hanover. Few people pretended at the time that a union on paper would automatically forge a united people. For many years after 1707, most Scottish people would not have noticed much difference.

As part of the new constitutional arrangements the Scots retained considerable autonomy, something that was denied to the Welsh after their union with England in 1536 and, to a lesser extent, to the Irish after they were absorbed into the United Kingdom in 1801. In particular, the Scots maintained a separate and very different legal system. The majority of Scots belonged to the Presbyterian church, which was very different in structure and doctrine from the Church of England. They also had a more comprehensive and sophisticated education system than the other countries of the British Isles. Lastly, the Gaelic language and culture remained strong in the Highlands and Western Isles, until dealt an almost terminal blow by the clearances (forced removals from the land) of the late eighteenth and early nineteenth centuries, which scattered native speakers across North America.

Many Scots, especially those from the middle classes, took advantage of the economic opportunities offered by England, and in particular London. Scottish migrants of all backgrounds came from a small and very poor country, where advancement was limited, as the unfavourable comments of eighteenth century observers show. Nevertheless, the Scots were able to capitalize on a superior educational system, which in the century after 1750, for example, trained 10,000 doctors. The Scots spread through the British Empire and beyond. Some 40,000 went to North America between 1760 and 1776. To run their affairs in western Canada, the Hudson's Bay Company recruited generations of Scots, particularly from the Orkney Islands.

The administration of Scotland

It was not until 1885 that the post of Secretary of State for Scotland, political head of a separate Scottish Office, was created. With the exception of Tom Johnston, who was Secretary of State during the Second World War, few of the occupants of the position can be regarded as distinguished. Before 1885 new civil service departments for Scotland – such as the General Register Office or GRO(S) – were created when required. After this date, many functions which in

England would have been undertaken by separate departments became the responsibility of the Scottish Office. Its records form the core of the National Archives of Scotland.

From the 1970s to the 1990s devolution was a big issue in Scotland. A referendum to devolve power to a Scottish Parliament only just failed to succeed in 1979. Nearly twenty years later, in 1997, a second vote was overwhelmingly in favour of devolution. A new Scottish Parliament, which took over most of the powers of the Scottish Office, met for the first time in 1999. It was the biggest change in Scotland's constitutional arrangements for almost 300 years.

On the surface local government in Scotland appears similar to that of England, but there are many differences. The main administrative areas before 1975 were the counties, burghs and parishes. The counties developed from the sheriffdoms of the Middle Ages. In the eighteenth century, and again in 1889, their boundaries were rationalized. Burghs were roughly equivalent to the English boroughs. The most important of these bodies were the royal burghs, which held a charter from the crown.

For most people living outside the burghs, the parish was the administrative area that most directly affected their lives. Parish administration had both religious and civil aspects, being concerned with ecclesiastical matters, such as religious observance and moral behaviour, as well as civil matters such as the provision of education and running the Poor Law. During the second half of the nineteenth century these civil matters were generally transferred to county councils and other authorities.

The old system was swept away in 1975, when nine regional councils and 56 district or island councils were established. There were further changes in 1996, when the old regions and districts were replaced by 29 unitary authorities, although separate island councils remained for Shetland, Orkney and the Western Isles.

GENERAL REGISTER OFFICE FOR SCOTLAND

Introduction

The basic sources for Scottish genealogical research are held by the General Register Office for Scotland. The holdings of the GRO(S) are conveniently summarized in a free leaflet (S1), *List of Main Records in the Care of the Registrar General*, which is available from the GRO(S) or can be downloaded from their website. Other, less immediately important, material is held by the National Archives of Scotland (NAS) – formerly the Scottish Record Office (SRO). Both bodies are to be found, conveniently close to each other, in Edinburgh. Material held by the NAS is discussed on page 22–29.

▼ **General Register Office for Scotland**
New Register House
3 West Register Street
Edinburgh EH1 3YT
Telephone: 0131 334 0380
Email: records@gro-scotland.gov.uk
Internet: http://www.gro-scotland.gov.uk

Search room opening hours:
9 a.m. to 4.30 p.m., Monday to Friday
(closed weekends and public holidays)

Disabled access is available. There are no restaurant facilities in the building, but there are a large number of restaurants and pubs a few minutes' walk away.

Charges for access

For a fee, any member of the public over the age of 16 can search the records held by the GRO(S). There is no free admission. The charges (current at time of publication) are:

- Part-day: £10 (available only after 1 p.m.)

- One day: £13 (purchased more than 14 days in advance)

- One day: £17

- One week: £65

If you have a number of Scottish ancestors, these charges can work out considerably cheaper than the English system of consulting the indexes free but paying for copies.

For more details, see GRO(S) leaflet S3, *Guidance for General Search Customers in New Register House*, which is available free of charge or can be downloaded from the GRO(S) website.

Scots Origins

It is now possible to get access to most of the records of the GRO(S) through the Scots Origins service, which is an online 'pay per view' database. The website contains fully searchable indexes for:

- old parish registers, 1553–1854

- statutory registers of births and marriages, 1855–99

- statutory registers of deaths, 1855–1924

- the 1891 census

An additional year of births, marriages and deaths data is added each year. Thus, in 2001 birth and marriage entries for 1900 and death registers for 1925 will be made available. A charge is made for the service. Full details are given on the website at http://www.origins.net.

What visitors cannot download are extracts from the records or certificates. You can order extracts from Scots Origins through the GRO(S). These will be sent to you by post and the cost of each one is £10. See above for details of how to contact the GRO(S).

Scots Origins can be a very useful tool. It might save you hours of research and a journey to Edinburgh.

Statutory registers of births, marriages and deaths

A national system of birth, marriage and death registration was only adopted in Scotland in 1855. Before then, events were imperfectly recorded in the old parish registers (OPRs). See page 19 for more about OPRs.

A rather different system was adopted in Scotland than in other parts of the British Isles. A network of registration districts, generally parishes, was created, with a registrar in each. It was his duty to record births, marriages and deaths. A copy of his register was to be kept locally, and another was to be sent to the General Register Office in Edinburgh.

The registers for the first year, 1855, contain rather more information than those for subsequent years. Protests about the amount of work needed for these detailed requirements, led to a simplification in 1856 and subsequently. Even so these registers are, in general, rather more informative than their English equivalents.

You can see these records at New Register House in Edinburgh, although local registrars should have registers for their district. The system at New Register House is rather different from that at the Family Records Centre in London. The indexes are available on computer and are easy to use. From the information given in the index you can select the microfiche containing the appropriate register. Each microfiche may contain a dozen or more pages from the register. You are free to note down the information on your ancestor contained in the register. You can also order a certified copy of the certificate, although it will not contain any additional information.

If you can't visit Edinburgh, the GRO(S) will send you a certified copy of the register entry. This currently costs £8 and takes about 10 to 14 days. The indexes are online via Scots Origins or can be accessed on the Scot Link service at the FRC.

The registers for 1855 give the following information:

- **birth registers:** ages and birthplaces of the parents; number of other children, whether living or deceased

- **marriage registers:** birthplaces of bride and groom; any children by former marriages, whether living or deceased

- **death registers:** place of birth of deceased; how long they had been living in the district where the death was recorded; the names and ages of any children living or deceased; place of burial; name of the undertaker

Birth registers give the following information from 1856 (items not on English certificates marked thus*):

- surname and forename of the child

- date and hour* of birth and the address where it took place

- child's sex

- father's name and occupation – if the father was not known, 'illegitimate' is stated*

- mother's name, with her maiden name and any former married names

- the date and place of their marriage*

- signature, designation and residence of the informant

Marriage registers give the following information from 1856 (items not on English certificates marked thus*):

- date and place of marriage. (Unlike in England, marriages could take place outside the church or register office. Indeed, during the nineteenth century marriage in church was rare. The usual location was the bride's home, but hotels were also popular.)

- signatures of the bridge and groom

- previous marital status of the bride and groom; and their relationship, if they were related to each other*

- their occupations and where they lived

- names of fathers and names of mothers*; fathers' occupations

- signature of officiating minister and two witnesses

- date of registration and signature of registrar

Death registers give the following information from 1856 (items not on English certificates marked thus*):

- full name – if the surname had been changed then both names had to be stated

- occupation, age and sex

- whether single, married or widowed

- the name of any spouse

- actual date and place, including time* of death

- names and occupation of the parents of the deceased*

- cause of death

- signature and qualification of the informant

In 1856 itself, not all of this information was included on certificates.

ⓘ **Remember**

Scots Origins (see p. 12) and Scot Link (see p. 31) are convenient ways of accessing Scottish records – including birth, marriage and death registers – without having to go to Edinburgh.

Census returns

Census returns for Scotland are very similar to their English and Welsh equivalents. The first Scottish census was in 1801. Thereafter censuses have been taken every 10 years, with the exception of 1941. Very few records survive for the 1801 to 1831 censuses. Censuses are available between 1841 and 1891, although the 1841 census is not as useful as later ones. The 1901 census will become available in January 2002.

As in England, Scotland was divided into enumeration districts containing about 200 houses. Each enumerator issued forms to houses in his (and from 1891 her) district, and collected them the day after the census. He or she then entered the details into enumeration books, which were sent to Edinburgh for analysis.

The layout of the form and the questions asked followed the English pattern closely. The only difference of note was the inclusion, in 1891, of a question asking whether Gaelic was spoken in the household. Persons born in England were normally noted simply as having been in the country, and it is quite rare to see the place of actual birth noted.

The census followed the English custom of calling women by their married names – although there are exceptions – rather than the Scottish tradition of women retaining their maiden name on marriage. It is important to remember that names were sometimes given in their formal form, e.g. Jane instead of Jean and Janet instead of Jessie.

A complete set of census returns is available at New Register House in Edinburgh. Copies for local areas are often to be found in local libraries or archives. Complete sets are also held by the Society of Genealogists in London. In addition, they can be ordered at Family History Centres. These are run by the Church of Jesus of Latter-day Saints (LDS Church) and can be contacted via:

▼ The Genealogical Society of Utah
British Isles Family History Service Centre
185 Penns Lane
Sutton Coldfield
West Midlands B76 8JU

Finding individuals in the census can be difficult unless you know an exact address. Fortunately there are complete surname indexes for the 1881 and 1891 censuses. The 1881 index is widely available on CD-ROM, as part of the British 1881 census surname index. The 1891 index, containing 4 million entries, is available on Scots Origins at http://www.origins.net. Census indexes before 1881 are listed in P. Ruthven-Murray, *Scottish Census Indexes: A Brief Guide to the Availability of Census Indexes 1841–1871 and Where to Find Them* (Association of Scottish Family History Societies, 1996).

The census nights were:	
1841	6 June
1851	30 March
1861	7 April
1871	2 April
1881	3 April
1891	5 April
1901	31 March

Old parish registers

Before the introduction of civil registration in 1855, the parish ministers or session clerks of the Presbyterian Church of Scotland in some 900 parishes kept these registers, which record births and baptisms, proclamation of banns and marriages, and deaths and burials. Although the GRO(S) has some 3,500 of these old parish registers, they are far from complete. The oldest register is for baptisms and banns at Errol, Perthshire, and dates from 1553; for some parishes the earliest registers are for the early nineteenth century. The reasons for this incompleteness are many, but they include the fact that by the late eighteenth century increasing numbers of people were turning to churches other than the established one and that, on occasion, a fee was charged for the registration of a baptism. In addition, standards of record-keeping vary considerably.

In short, these records are not dissimilar to English parish registers, which may also be incomplete and poorly kept. The fascinating history of OPRs is described in Cecil Sinclair, *Jock Tamson's Bairns* (GRO(S), 2000).

There is now, however, a comprehensive index to baptisms and marriages *only*. It contains 9.7 million entries. Copies are available on microfiche at New Register House, the Society of

Genealogists in London and other libraries in Scotland. It is available as a separate disk in the FamilySearch CD-ROM series at the FRC. It is also in searchable database form on the Scots Origins website (see p. 18).

For baptisms, most OPRs contain the following information:

- date of the baptism, often with the date of birth

- name of father and mother (often with her maiden name)

- names of witnesses with their occupations (common in earlier registers)

- whether the child was illegitimate (usually referred to as 'born in fornication') and the name of the father, where known

For marriages and banns, most OPRs only tell you:

- date of the event

- names of the parties being married

- occasionally, the name of the bride's father

Finding the death or burial of an individual in the old parish registers is particularly frustrating, because entries for deaths vary greatly. Indeed, on occasion they may be little more than an account of people borrowing the mort-cloth used in the funeral ceremony. This can be overcome to some extent by using inscriptions on gravestones and memorials. A large collection of these monumental inscriptions is at New Register House. Local studies libraries may have sets for their area.

> **ⓘ Remember**
> Although the information contained in OPRs is variable and often incomplete, they can nevertheless be useful for basic details of births, baptisms, marriages and deaths before 1855, when a national system of civil registration was adopted in Scotland.

Other records at New Register House

There are small collections of other registers that might be of use to readers. The registers of events outside the United Kingdom are known as the 'Minor Records':

- **Register of neglected entries.** Births, marriages and deaths known to have occurred between 1801 and 1854 but not included in the OPRs.

- **Marine register of births and deaths after 1855.** Births and deaths on British ships where the baby's father or the deceased was Scottish.

- **Service records after 1881.** Births, marriages and deaths of Scottish persons serving in the armed forces.

- **War registers.** Three registers for the South African (Boer) War (1899–1902) and the two world wars, listing Scottish men who died while serving. Officers do not appear in the registers for the First World War, while the register for the Second World War is incomplete. The information in these registers is quite detailed, and can supplement service records and other material available at the PRO.

- **Consular returns.** Certified copies of registrations relating to persons of Scottish descent or birth made by British consuls. Records of births and deaths date from 1914, marriages from 1917.

- **Foreign countries (1860–1965).** Until the end of 1965 registers of births of children with Scottish parents and of marriages and deaths of Scottish people were compiled, based on information supplied by the parties themselves.

- **Registers of still births.** These registers begin in 1939 and are not open to the public.

- **Registers of adoptions.** These registers begin in 1930.

- **Registers of divorces.** These registers begin in May 1984 and relate to divorces granted in Scottish courts.

NATIONAL ARCHIVES OF SCOTLAND

The National Archives of Scotland (formerly the Scottish Record Office) is the equivalent of the Public Record Office north of the border. In some ways its collections are more comprehensive than those of the PRO, because it holds many local records and private papers, which in England would be with local archives. On the other hand, the NAS has very little about great matters of state outside Scotland.

The NAS has two search rooms in Edinburgh, about a mile apart from each other.

The **Historical Search Room**, at General Register House, is probably the most useful place to start. Here, you can consult:

- the records of the pre-Union Scottish government and Parliament

- Privy Council records

- testaments

- church records

- burgh records

- records relating to sale and purchase of land and property

- the register of deeds

- collections of family, legal and estate records

The **West Search Room**, at West Register House, is for readers consulting:

- maps and plans

- railway and ship-building records

- court records

- records of the Scottish Office

The addresses of the two search rooms are:

▶ **Historical Search Room**
General Register House
Princes Street
Edinburgh

West Search Room
West Register House
Charlotte Square
Edinburgh

The contact address of the National Archives of Scotland is:

▼ **National Archives of Scotland**
HM General Register House
Edinburgh EH1 3YY
Telephone: 0131 535 1334
Email: enquiries@nas.gov.uk.

Both search rooms are open between 9 a.m. and 4.45 p.m., Mondays to Fridays. They are closed at weekends and on public holidays, and for a period in November for stocktaking. New readers need to apply for a reader's ticket, for which proof of identity is required. Tickets are valid for three years and can be used in either reading room.

The NAS has the same 30-year rule as the Public Record Office, which means in general that records less than 30 years old are not made available to the public. Certain records, particularly those relating to individuals, may be closed for a longer period, generally 75 years. All the records described in this guide, however, are open without restriction.

As some material is stored at an out-station, it is important to check in advance that the records you are interested in are available and where they can be seen, by contacting the NAS.

The best and most comprehensive guide to the National Archives is Cecil Sinclair, *Tracing Your Scottish Ancestors* (2nd edn., HMSO, 1990). Most books on Scottish family history describe the main holdings.

The main types of records likely to be of use in your research are described below. They can be consulted in the Historical Search Room at General Register House.

Nonconformist registers

Confusingly, although the parish registers of the Church of Scotland before 1855 are with the General Register Office for Scotland, their nonconformist equivalents are at the National Archives. As in England, the vast majority of Scottish people were members of the established church, but by the end of the eighteenth century an increasing minority were looking elsewhere for spiritual inspiration. In part this was the result of groups of the faithful breaking away from the church. The Disruption of 1843 was the largest and most important of these movements, and it saw the creation of the Free Church of Scotland ('the wee frees', as they are sometimes known). Registers of this church and of the United Presbyterian Church up to 1855 are at the NAS. The NAS also has photocopies of many pre-1855 Roman Catholic registers and some records for the Quakers and the Methodist, Episcopal, Congregational and Unitarian churches. Post-1855 records for all these churches are likely to be either with the local record office or with the church itself.

Testaments and inventories

The big difference between wills and their Scottish equivalents – testaments – is that testaments are restricted to moveable property. Heritable property, that is land and buildings, is covered by retours or services of heirs, which are described below. These records are easy to use because they are indexed, in good condition and fairly easy to read.

Technically, a testament is the legal device confirming the appointment of an executor to administer the moveable property of the deceased, whether he or she made a will or not. Each testament gives the name of the deceased, usually the date of death, the confirmation of the executor, and an inventory (or list) of the moveable property of the deceased (which may include household furniture, implements of trade and debts owed to and by the deceased). There may also be a copy of the will itself.

Up to 1822 all testaments were confirmed by ecclesiastical Commissary Courts. These were held in Aberdeen, Argyll, Brechin, Caithness, Dumfries, Dunblane, Dunkeld, Edinburgh, Glasgow, Hamilton and Campsie, Inverness, the Isles, Kirkcudbright, Lanark, Lauder, Moray, Orkney and Shetland, Peebles, Ross, St Andrews, Stirling and Wigtown. The exact boundaries are shown on maps in C. Humphrey-Smith, *Phillimore Atlas and Index of Parish Registers* (Phillimore, 1993). These courts dealt with testaments for their own area, although Edinburgh took testaments from the whole of Scotland, as well as for Scots who died abroad. Microfilm copies of the indexes to testaments, arranged by court, are at the Society of Genealogists in London.

In 1823 this work was taken over by the Sheriff Courts. Each court undertook this business in a slightly different way. Once you have identified the place where the testament was confirmed, it is best to seek advice on how to order the appropriate record. Between 1876 and 1959, however, the task is somewhat easier, for there is an annual set of indexes called the *Calendar of Confirmation and Inventories*. The Calendar includes all persons whose executors have been confirmed, in alphabetical order. Married women are indexed only under their married name. Each entry gives the name of the deceased, the date and place of death, where and when confirmation was granted, the name of the executor, and the value of the estate. From this information, it is a fairly easy task to look up the testament in the records of the appropriate court.

For a more detailed description of testaments and how to use the records at the NAS, see Sinclair, *Tracing Your Scottish Ancestors*, chapter 6.

Testament tips

1. Very few people left a will. The property of the deceased was normally shared out amongst members of the family.

2. Some records have been lost due to fire and other accidents.

3. As the eldest son inherited all the heritable property (that is, the land and buildings) of his deceased father, he did not receive any of the moveable property, so his name may not appear in the testament.

4. If the deceased died in debt, the next-of-kin might not wish to take on his debts. In cases such as this, it is not uncommon for a creditor to be named as executor and for the testament to contain no genealogical information.

5. Testaments are normally, though not always, confirmed within a year of death.

6. The NAS also has Estate Duty Records from 1804, but they are unlikely to tell you more than you have discovered from testament records.

Retours or services of heirs

Until 1868 land or buildings – known as heritable property – could not be left in a will. Inheritances of this type of property were recorded in the retours, or services of heirs. Special retours named the property, while general retours did not. Other details to be found in these records are the names of the heir and the deceased, their relationship, and possibly the date of death. Retours begin in 1547 and were written in Latin until 1847, except for the years 1652–9. The originals are at the NAS, but indexes (in English) may be found in large reference libraries in Scotland. Retours are covered in more detail in Sinclair, *Tracing Your Scottish Ancestors*, chapter 7.

Sasines

One of the most important sources held at the NAS are the registers of sasines, which record the transfer of land and houses from 1617. There is no English equivalent. If your ancestors owned even the smallest piece of land or cottage, you should find something in these registers. The bequest of land within families may help you establish family relationships. Even if no family links are established, there will be information about the location of the property, the size of any land, and the occupations of the vendor and purchaser.

From 1617 to 1868 there was a general register, recording property throughout Scotland, and various particular registers for each county. In addition royal burghs had their own registers. As a result, you may need to check in three different places. From 1869 registers were kept in each county, although burghs continued to maintain their own records until the middle of the twentieth century. The registers were kept until fairly recently, when they were replaced by registration of title.

Most sasines are at the NAS, but registers for Aberdeen, Dundee (both before 1809) and Glasgow are held by local record offices. The Society of Genealogists has copies of a few indexes to burgh registers of sasines. Sasines are described in depth in Sinclair, *Tracing Your Scottish Ancestors*, chapter 8.

Kirk Session records

Each Church of Scotland parish had its own Kirk Session, which administered the affairs of the parish and dealt with most aspects of people's lives. A great deal of information can therefore be found in session books, including reports on the misconduct of parishioners on the Sabbath – particularly fornication. These records also deal with the relief offered to poor members of the parish, the appointment of school-masters and other employees, and the loan of burial clothes. Many session books are at the NAS, while others are at local record offices. A number of these books have been transcribed and published.

ⓘ **Remember**

Before 1868, testaments (the Scottish equivalent of wills) were restricted to moveable property; details of heritable property (land and buildings) were recorded in retours or services of heirs.

FAMILY RECORDS CENTRE

The Family Records Centre in London has many records that may contain details of Scottish ancestors who moved south. The Centre also has Scot Link, a dedicated computer link to the GRO(S) in Edinburgh.

The FRC is a service for family historians, set up in 1997 by the Office for National Statistics (ONS) and the Public Record Office (PRO). It provides a comprehensive reference resource, including indexes to the major sources for family history in the United Kingdom, microfilm copies of a wide range of documents (including the census for England and Wales), CD-ROMs, online search facilities, and a large collection of reference books, indexes and maps.

No original documents are kept at the FRC. You can see the originals of *some* categories of material (but not the census) at the PRO at Kew. For a guide to the FRC, see J. Cox, *Never Been Here Before?* (PRO, 1998).

▼ **Family Records Centre**
  1 Myddelton Street
  London EC1R 1UW
  Telephone: 020 8392 5300
  Telephone for birth, marriage and
  death certificates: 0151 471 4800
  Fax: 020 8392 5307
  Internet: http://www.pro.gov.uk/frc/

You can visit the FRC in person without an appointment. If you are disabled and require parking, phone first, as disabled parking places must be booked in advance.

Opening times (closed Sundays and public holidays):

Monday	9 a.m to 5 p.m.
Tuesday	10 a.m. to 7 p.m.
Wednesday	9 a.m. to 5 p.m.
Thursday	9 a.m. to 7 p.m.
Friday	9 a.m. to 5 p.m.
Saturday	9.30 a.m. to 5 p.m.

Birth, marriage and death records after 1 July 1837

The births, marriage and death records held at the FRC are only for England and Wales. The indexes are on the ground floor. Scottish records, which begin in 1855, are available in Edinburgh.

Scot Link

The indexes to records at the General Register Office (Scotland) can be searched using the Scot Link facility on the ground floor at the FRC, for a fee (currently £4 for half an hour), but certificates have to be ordered from Edinburgh. The service gives access to online indexes to the birth, marriage and death registers from 1 January 1855, including adoptions from 1930 and divorces from May 1984. It also accesses the computerized indexes of all the names in the old parish registers of baptisms and marriages between 1553 and 1854, and surname indexes to the Scottish census returns for 1881 and 1891. A partial service is also available over the internet at http://www.origins.net (see pp. 12–13).

It is not easy to identify the Scottish ancestry of people described in the birth, marriage and death certificates at the

FRC. Only from 1969 did parents of newborn children have to supply their place of birth. Death certificates, but not the indexes to them, give the date and place of birth of the deceased.

Unlike in Scotland, users of the English system cannot see the original certificates at the FRC. To obtain a certificate, you need to consult the registers to find the correct reference. The document can then be either collected a few days later or posted to you. At the time of writing, the cost of each certificate is £6.50.

For more about English and Welsh certificates, see *Using Birth, Marriage and Death Records* (PRO, 2000).

Armed forces returns

On the ground floor of the FRC you will find various registers for the armed forces, including Army registers of births and marriages 1761–1965 and of deaths 1796–1965, both in the UK and abroad. From 1796 there are the Army chaplains' returns of births, marriages and deaths for soldiers serving abroad. These records include men who served in Scottish regiments. This series of registers also includes the Royal Navy from 1881 and the Royal Air Force from 1920. They are indexed, although you will have to have a rough idea of when an event occurred. In addition, there are indexes to men who died while serving in the forces during the two world wars and the Boer War. It is important to be aware that the GRO(S) also has records relating to Scottish service personnel, including returns of births, marriages and deaths of Scottish persons at military stations abroad between 1881 and 1959.

Census returns

The census reveals that considerable numbers of Scottish people lived in England and Wales. In 1871 the authorities found 213,254 people born in Scotland south of the border – of whom 113,889 were men and 99,365 women. Fortunately it can be relatively easy to track them down, although there can be pitfalls. It helps if you know where they were living at about the time of the census, which was normally taken in April. The earliest census to be kept is the 1841 census. The latest one available is for 1891. The 1901 census will be opened on 2 January 2002.

Census records can be consulted on the first floor at the FRC. English and Welsh census returns are very similar to their Scottish counterparts and contain much the same information – that is, name, age, marital status, relationship to head of household, occupation, and place of birth. All censuses thus identify individuals born in Scotland. The 1841 census only indicates whether somebody was born north of the border. Even in later censuses, it is unusual for the exact town or county to be given, which can be frustrating.

Census records are arranged by enumeration districts within registration districts or sub-districts (i.e. they are arranged by place rather than name). Surname and street indexes, where they exist, can help you to track down an individual. There are name indexes for the whole of the 1881 census, for most of the one held in 1851, and for parts of the other censuses. The 1881 census index is on CD-ROM and is readily available at libraries around the country and the FRC. A surname index for the whole of the 1901 census will be made available when these records are released in January 2002. In addition, there are a number of street indexes to London and large towns and cities – which can make searching considerably easier if you know the name of the street where an ancestor lived at about the time of the census.

For more about census records, see *Using Census Records* (PRO, 2000).

Nonconformist registers

Also available at the FRC are nonconformist records. By the time of the introduction of national registration of births, marriages and deaths in 1837, perhaps a quarter of the population did not belong to the Church of England. The law said that baptisms, marriages and burials had to be performed by Anglican churches, although by the end of the eighteenth century this was widely ignored. Nonconformists (also called dissenters) preferred their own Baptist, Congregational or, above all, Methodist chapels. With the introduction of national registration, nonconformist chapels were asked to send their registers to the government, and these records were eventually transferred to the PRO. Microfilm copies can be seen at the FRC and the PRO. Note that there are very few Catholic registers amongst this material.

As most Scots in England before 1837 were officially dissenters, there are registers for a number of kirks in London and elsewhere of the various Scottish ceremonies. These records have been indexed and the information added to the *International Genealogical Index (IGI)*, a name index to worldwide genealogical sources compiled by the LDS Church (see p. 18). You can use the *IGI* on the internet at http://www.familysearch.org. Both the SoG and the LDS Church have copies of these registers.

For further information about these registers, see *Using Birth, Marriage and Death Records* (PRO, 2000)

Wills

Unlike the centralized system of proving testaments in Scotland, the English system before 1858 was chaotic, with a choice of places in which wills could be proved. The most important of these courts, because it covered the whole of England and Wales, was the Prerogative Court of Canterbury (PCC). The wills of wealthy Scottish merchants based in London, or even in the colonies, may have been proved in the PCC. It wasn't just the wealthy who used this court, either: it was not uncommon for soldiers and sailors to have their wills proved there.

Most PCC wills have been indexed, and these indexes are available at the FRC, the PRO and the SoG. At the Society of Genealogists, there are lists of Scottish people whose wills were proved in the PCC. Copies of PCC wills are also available at the PRO at Kew.

English wills can be tricky to use. The staff at the FRC can help you and there are a number of pamphlets explaining the intricacies of the system, including *Using Wills* (PRO, 2000).

Tip
Don't be surprised to find that PCC calendars refer to Scotland as North Britain.

PUBLIC RECORD OFFICE

The Public Record Office is the national archive of the United Kingdom – and England and Wales. The PRO has records created or acquired by the central government in Whitehall and the central law courts over more than 900 years. As explained above, Scotland has its own national archives in Edinburgh, which has records of purely Scottish interest. As a result, the PRO is not the first place to visit when searching for Scottish ancestors. That said, there is material about many Scotsmen (and a few Scotswomen) at the PRO. For a guide to family history records at the PRO, see A. Bevan, *Tracing Your Ancestors in the Public Record Office*, 5th edn (PRO, 1999).

▼ **Public Record Office**
   Kew
   Richmond
   Surrey TW9 4DU
   General telephone: 020 8876 3444
   Telephone number for enquiries: 020 8392 5200
   Internet: http://www.pro.gov.uk/

Opening times (closed Sundays and Bank Holidays):

Monday	9 a.m. to 5 p.m.
Tuesday	10 a.m. to 7 p.m.
Wednesday	9 a.m. to 5 p.m.
Thursday	9 a.m. to 7 p.m.
Friday	9 a.m. to 5 p.m.
Saturday	9 a.m. to 5 p.m.

No appointment is needed to visit the PRO in Kew, but you will need a reader's ticket to gain access to the research areas.

To obtain a ticket you need to take with you a full UK driving licence or a UK banker's card or a passport if you are a British citizen, and your passport or national identity card if you are not. Note that the last time for ordering documents is 4 p.m. on Mondays, Wednesdays and Fridays; 4.30 p.m. on Tuesdays and Thursdays; and 2.30 p.m. on Saturdays.

Records at the PRO are normally kept together according to the government department that created them. Departments are given prefixes that help you to identify them. The War Office, for example, is WO and the Foreign Office is FO. Within each department, similar types of records form separate series. Each of these series is assigned a unique number. Thus the series WO 95, for example, contains war diaries of the First World War; WO 96, militia attestation papers; and WO 97, soldiers' documents between 1760 and 1913. Within each series, each 'piece' – normally a file or volume – is given a unique reference. For example, WO 95/1263 is a First World War war diary for the 1st Battalion of the Black Watch. It is this three-part reference that you order, and need to quote in correspondence or in any book.

For most popular family history searches at the PRO, simple explanatory leaflets are available. These will guide you step-by-step to your reference. To make a search not covered by these leaflets, you will need to use the PRO's catalogue. Traditionally, references were looked up in the paper catalogue, which lists every piece in each series. This paper version has largely been superseded by the electronic catalogue, which can be searched by subject. Thus it is now easy to find, for example, the 450 references to the Black Watch by typing this phrase into the computer. The electronic catalogue is also available through the PRO's website. Paper and electronic versions of the catalogue are available at Kew.

Records relating to Scotland and the Scots can be found in many places. There are some 280 series of records and 24,000 individual pieces alone that have Scotland, Scottish or Scots in the title, although it has to be said that relatively few of these entries are likely to be of immediate use to family historians. On the other hand, there are many records not specifically labelled as 'Scottish' that contain material of interest to researchers tracing ancestors from north of the border.

The sources listed below are those most likely to contain records relating to individual Scots.

Military records

The fallen of two world wars

The Commonwealth War Graves Commission was set up to commemorate the dead of the First World War, and has done its best to find and record as many war deaths of British and Commonwealth men as possible from 1914 to the present. It is perhaps best known for the hundreds of carefully tended, and very moving, cemeteries scattered through northern France and Belgium. Its database is now online at http://www.cwgc.org and will tell you where a man is buried, when he died, and the unit he served with. You can also write to the Commonwealth War Graves Commission, 2 Marlow Road, Maidenhead SL6 7DX, or phone 01628 34221.

For the First World War, most of the officers and other ranks are recorded in *Soldiers Died in the Great War*.

Originally this was a multi-volume book, but it has recently been put onto CD-ROM, which makes it very easy to search. The information contained about individuals varies and is not always accurate, but it will indicate where a man died, his rank, and the regiment he was with. It may also tell you where and when a man enlisted and his age at enlistment. Copies can be used at the PRO and at the library of the Society of Genealogists (SoG).

There is a roll of honour for men who died in the Second World War at the PRO in series WO 304. This too is now available on CD-ROM. Copies can be used in the PRO and SoG libraries.

The Army in particular was popular with many young Scotsmen who wanted to escape home and see something of the world. Early on they acquired a reputation for bravery – during the First World War, German soldiers called the Highland regiments 'devils in skirts' in tribute to their fighting spirit. It was not only poor 'Jocks' from the Highland glens and Glasgow slums who joined up; the army was equally attractive to the upper classes. In the mid-eighteenth century about a quarter of the officers in the British Army came from Scotland; and although the proportion later declined, the Scots continued to provide a large number of officers and leading generals. These included James Murray, the first British governor of Canada, and Douglas Haig, commander of the British forces during the First World War.

The Public Record Office has service records for men who left the forces before the end of 1920. Whether you are looking for the records of a serviceman or an officer, it can help if you know roughly when he was in the forces and the regiment, ship or unit he served with.

There were, and still are, a number of specific Scottish Highland or Lowland regiments. They were treated in exactly the same way as their English, Welsh or Irish counterparts, although some allowance was made in dress and the use of bagpipes. It was customary before the First World War for regiments to recruit primarily within a local district, but this did not prevent non-Scots from joining Highland units and some Scots joined English regiments. The link with locality was, however, effectively broken during the two world wars, when the needs of war meant that considerable numbers of non-Scots were assigned to Scottish regiments.

It is important to recognize the difference between officers, non-commissioned officers (NCOs) and other ranks (ratings in the Navy). NCOs and ordinary soldiers, sailors and airmen made up the vast majority of the armed forces. Their records will be found in different series from those of officers. Officers are also listed in published *Army Lists*, *Navy Lists* and *Air Force Lists*, and it is often possible to trace the outlines of their careers from these publications. Service records vary greatly in format, but they all contain roughly the same information.

The GRO(S) in Edinburgh has some records relating to Scottish service personnel. These include records of deaths in the two world wars, and returns of births, marriages and deaths of Scottish persons at military stations abroad between 1881 and 1959 (see p. 32).

Army

Officers

From 1740 all officers were listed in the published *Army List*, which appeared at least annually. If your ancestor is not in the *List*, then he was not an officer. There was a private rival publication between 1839 and 1915 – *Hart's Army List* – which can contain biographical information, particularly about the campaigns officers served in. Both series can be consulted at Kew.

For the nineteenth century there are several different series of records detailing the service of officers. Fortunately the PRO holds an alphabetical card index to these records.

All officers receive a royal commission. The PRO has correspondence about the purchase and sale of commissions between 1793 and 1871 (WO 31). This contains a great deal of valuable genealogical material.

Before 1871 officers went on half-pay when they retired – that is, they were paid a pension although they were, in theory at least, ready to be called up at any time. Retired officers continued to be listed in the *Army Lists*. There are registers and correspondence about the payment of pensions up to 1921, including some records for pensions paid to widows and children.

Service records for the First World War are now available at the PRO. About 85 per cent of these have survived, but they can be disappointing because they are often just about pension claims.

Other ranks

Before the 1880s, it is very helpful to know the regiment that the soldier served with. This can be difficult to discover. It may sometimes be possible to identify it from buttons or insignia on uniforms in old photographs. Alternatively, a man may simply have joined the regiment stationed near to where he lived. Records of the effects of dead soldiers are arranged alphabetically and these may help identify a regiment.

Especially useful are the soldiers' documents in WO 97, which are service records for men who received a pension between 1760 and 1913. There are few records before 1790. Before 1883 they are arranged by regiment. However, the Friends of the PRO have indexed the soldiers' documents up to 1854 by surname, and this index is available in the Microfilm Reading Room at Kew. The documents indicate when and where a man served, promotions, disciplinary offences, place and age on enlistment, and reason for discharge. They also often list wives and children.

Up to two-thirds of the Army service records for the period between 1914 and the end of 1920 were destroyed in the Second World War. Those documents that survived are in series WO 363 and are in the process of being microfilmed in surname order. The project should be completed by May 2002. In the meantime, the enquiry helpline on 020 8392 5300 will tell you which surnames have been microfilmed. The records contain the place and date of enlistment, medical details, disciplinary record and other information, although what is in each document varies greatly. There is also a series of service records, in WO 364, for men who received a pension after the First World War (for long service or medical discharge). What these records don't tell you much about is the experience of the man at the front. For this, you will need to consult the battalion war diaries in WO 95 (although these do not usually mention individuals by name).

An alternative source is the muster rolls, which list every man in a regiment (including officers) and were compiled monthly. They indicate a man's pay, offences committed during the previous month, and the location of the regiment. They begin in 1732 and end in 1898.

Men who had served the period of enlistment or been wounded were entitled to a pension from Chelsea Hospital. There are a variety of records to help. Most men were out-pensioners – that is, they received a pension at home – rather than in-pensioners, who lived in the hospital itself.

Officers and men also appear on campaign medal rolls, which before 1913 are in WO 100. During the First World War almost all men who served in the Army were entitled to at least two campaign medals. The medal record cards at the PRO will tell you which regiment(s) a man served with, which medals he was entitled to, and approximately when and where he served.

For more information about Army service records, see *Using Army Records* (PRO, 2000) or S. Fowler and W. Spencer, *Army Service Records for Family Historians* (PRO, 1998).

Royal Air Force and Royal Navy

Neither the Royal Air Force nor the Royal Navy differentiated recruits from Scotland in any way. For the RAF, the service records generally cover those who served in the First World

War. Records for those who served after 1919 (airmen and women) and the mid-1920s (officers) are still with the Ministry of Defence. Records of officers are in AIR 76 and other ranks in AIR 79.

Records for the Navy can be difficult to use. There are no service records for ratings until 1853. Men were discharged at the end of each voyage, so there is no continuity of service. You need to know the names of the ships an individual served with, which may include time in the merchant navy. The only really useful sources are ships' muster books and, to a lesser extent, logbooks.

In 1853 continuous service engagement books were introduced, and these formed the basis of service records until 1923. The information contained in these registers is by no means as full as in the Army equivalents, but they should enable you to find dates of entry and discharge, ships served on, promotions, disciplinary records, and some personal details. These records are in series ADM 139 and ADM 188.

Officers' service records are in some ways similar to their Army equivalents. All naval officers are listed in the *Navy List*, published at least annually. Service registers are in series ADM 196, and most entries are in the period between 1840 and 1920 – although there are some retrospective entries back as far as 1756 and deaths up to 1966 are also noted. These records will give you the ships served on, promotions, some personal details, and the name of any spouse.

Medal rolls for both gallantry and campaign medals are in ADM 171. They include awards for the First World War. Ships' logbooks are another useful source, although they rarely mention individuals. They are in ADM 53.

Royal Marine service records are fairly easy to use, although you will need to know which division a man served with (that is, Chatham, Plymouth, Portsmouth or Woolwich). Service records for other ranks between 1759 and 1918 are in ADM 159. Officers' service records are exactly the same as for their Naval counterparts.

For further information on the RAF, see William Spencer, *Air Force Records for Family Historians* (PRO, 2000). For more on the Royal Navy, see *Using Navy Records* (PRO, 2000); and for the Royal Marines, see Garth Thomas, *Records of the Royal Marines* (PRO, 1995).

Merchant seamen

Records of merchant seamen and shipping can be tricky to use, partly because the survival of records tends to be patchy, but mainly because there was no central registry of merchant seamen until 1913, apart from the period between 1835 and 1857. As a result, you may need to search a variety of record series.

The Merchant Shipping Act of 1835 ordered the registration of merchant seamen. Registers of seamen, and associated indexes, were kept between 1835 and 1857 and are now in series BT 112, BT 119 and BT 120. In addition, there are registers containing applications for seamen's tickets between 1845 and 1853 in BT 113. All these registers contain some personal details, such as age and place of birth, and indicate which ships a man served on.

The central registry was abandoned in 1857. It was not until 1913 that a new Central Index Register was established. This lasted until 1941, although many of the records for the period

1913–20 have been destroyed. Index cards for individuals, which include photographs as well as the usual personal details, are on microfiche at the PRO in series BT 348–350 and BT 364.

There are certificates of competency for masters and mates of ships, 1845–1921 (BT 122–127); engineers, 1862–1921 (BT 139–142); and skippers and mates of fishing boats, 1883–1930 (BT 129, BT 130, BT 138). After 1910 a combined index was started (BT 352). These index cards cover the period up to 1930 (though there are some entries beyond this date) and give name, place and year of birth, date and place of issue of certificate, and rank examined. Deaths, injuries and retirement are often mentioned. Applications for certificates up to 1928 are at the National Maritime Museum. After this, the system changed and there are no equivalent documents.

From 1747 ships were supposed to maintain lists of personnel on board. However, few of these musters survive before 1835, when they were replaced by agreements and crew lists. Masters of ships of more than 80 tons had to enter into a written agreement with each crew member about conditions of service. Copies had to be sent to the Registrar General of Shipping and Seamen, together with lists of crew members (which include some personal details) and often, from 1850, ships' logs. For the period between 1835 and 1857, these records are in BT 98. After 1857 they can be found in series BT 99, BT 144 and BT 165. However, after 1861 the PRO has only a 10 per cent sample. The remaining crew lists are scattered at the National Maritime Museum, the Memorial University of Newfoundland and various record offices, including a small number for Scottish ships at the National Archives of Scotland and Glasgow City Archives.

The relevant addresses are:

▼ **Maritime Research Centre**
National Maritime Museum
Greenwich
London SE10 9NF
Telephone: 020 8312 6691
Internet: http://www.nmm.ac.uk

▼ **Maritime History Archive**
Memorial University of Newfoundland
St John's, Newfoundland A1C 5S7
Canada
Internet: http://www.mun.ca/mha

For more on merchant navy records, see K. Smith, C. Watts and M. Watts, *Records of Merchant Shipping and Seamen* and C. Watts and M. Watts, *My Ancestor was a Merchant Seaman.*

Emigration

Many hundreds of thousands of people emigrated around the world from Scotland. The United States and Canada were favourite destinations. Unfortunately there are very few official records of their departure, and in most cases the authorities in the countries where they settled are likely to have better records of their arrival.

There are occasional exceptions, however, such as a register of emigrants to North America between 1773 and 1776, which can be found in series T 47. There is also, in CO 385/2 and AO 3/144, a list of 757 settlers enrolling for emigration to Canada at Edinburgh in 1815.

Scottish men and women were among those transported to Australia between 1788 and 1867. Details appear in the convict transportation registers in series HO 11, which provides the name of the ship on which the convict sailed, as well as the date and place of conviction and the term of the sentence. Some records about transportation of men convicted in Scottish courts are at the NAS. There is also other material on transportation, including petitions from wives seeking to accompany their husbands.

Outwards passenger lists between 1890 and 1960 are lists of passengers leaving Britain by sea for destinations outside Europe and the Mediterranean. They give the name, age, occupation and previous address of passengers. These lists are arranged by year and port, and can be found in BT 27. Because of the quantity of these records, it is almost essential to know approximately when and where a person left and the ship they went on. In addition, some lists are missing.

It may be possible to find details of the emigration of individuals – or, much more probably, groups of emigrants – in Colonial Office correspondence with various colonies and Foreign Office correspondence with British representatives abroad.

▼ **National Archives of Canada**
   395 Wellington Street
   Ottawa, Ontario K1A 0N3
   Internet: http//www.archives.ca

▼ **National Archives and Record Administration**
   700 Pennsylvania Avenue, N.W.
   Washington, DC 20408
   Internet: http//www.nara.gov

▼ **National Archives of New Zealand**
  10 Mulgrave Street
  Thorndon, Wellington
  Interent: http://www.archives.gov.nz

▼ **National Archives of Australia**
  Queen Victoria Terrace
  Parkes ACT 2600
  Internet: http://www.aa.gov.au

Further reading

There is no comprehensive introduction to emigration records, although the PRO will publish Roger Kershaw's guide to the subject in early 2002. There is, however, a good section on the subject in Bevan, *Tracing Your Ancestors*.

There are also a number of published lists of Scottish emigrants including:

David Dobson, *Directory of Scottish Settlers in North America 1625–1825* (6 vols, Genealogical Publishing Company, Baltimore, 1984)

W. Filby and M. Meyer (eds), *Passenger and Immigration Lists Index*, volumes of which have been published every year since 1983.

Donald Whyte, *A Dictionary of Scottish Emigrants to the USA* (2 vols, Magna Carta Book Company, Baltimore, 1972)

Donald Whyte, *A Dictionary of Scottish Emigration to Canada before Confederation* (Ontario Genealogical Society, 1986)

Copies of these books can be found at the Society of Genealogists and the Scottish Genealogy Society Library in Edinburgh.

The Hudson's Bay Company

The Hudson's Bay Company traded in the undeveloped lands of northern and western Canada, exporting animal skins, particularly beaver, to Europe and importing goods for sale to the native peoples. The Company was founded in 1670 and is still in business, although today it is largely known for running a chain of Canadian department stores. Many of its employees came from Scotland, especially from the Orkney Islands.

For nearly three centuries, the headquarters of the Company was in London. It was transferred to Winnipeg in the late 1960s, along with its archives. As a condition of allowing the export of its records, the company had to provide the PRO with a microfilm copy, which is now in series BH 1. The original material is held by the Provincial Archives of Manitoba, 200 Vaughan Street, Winnipeg, R3C 1T5, Canada. The website of these archives (http://www.gov.mb.ca/chc/archives/hbca) contains some useful pages about this collection.

Among the records in BH 1 are the headquarters' records (including minute books, which may record the appointment of staff), records concerning individual trading posts and logbooks, and papers relating to ships in the service of the company. These records are not easy to use and there are no central staff registers. Before you start, you should at least know roughly when an ancestor served with the company, as well as where he was based.

Immigration

Until about 1905 the government was unconcerned about people coming to Britain. Provided they didn't cause trouble, anybody could settle in Britain. As a result, there are very few records about immigration. Immigrants should, of course, appear on the census if they arrived before 1891, although it is unusual for information other than their country of birth to appear in the census enumerators' books.

The best source is probably the lists of people who became naturalized or sought denization, which was in effect a legal half-way house to naturalization. Before the First World War it was relatively uncommon for immigrants to become British citizens. Generally, you only did this if you wanted to own land. Before 1844 naturalization required a private Act of Parliament, but in 1844 the procedure was simplified and the numbers of people naturalized increased sharply. An index to those naturalized is attached to the catalogue for record series H O1.

Incoming passenger lists, in series BT 26, begin in 1878. As with outgoing passenger lists (see pp. 47–9), they are only for people who arrived by sea at British ports from outside Europe and the Mediterranean. The same difficulties apply, so you need to know approximately when and where, and on which ship, a person arrived.

Scotland has a large Polish community, whose members mainly arrived after the Second World War. The records of the Polish Resettlement Corps are in WO 315. This was set up in 1946 to ease Polish ex-servicemen's transition to civilian life in Britain. There are other types of material in

AST 7, AST 11 and AST 18. Many of these records are in Polish and most files on individuals are closed for 75 years.

For more about immigration records, see R. Kershaw and M. Pearsal, *Immigrants and Aliens: A Guide to Sources on UK Immigration and Citizenship* (PRO, 2000).

Some other sources

A number of Scots joined the Metropolitan Police in London. The authorities thought highly of the honesty and probity of the Scottish recruits in the early days, when constables were frequently discharged for misconduct, including drunkenness. Service records are to be found in series MEPO 4 and go from 1829 to about 1909, although there are some gaps. Pension records to 1932 are in series MEPO 21.

Among the oddest collections of records at the PRO of use to the family historian are the registers of habitual drunkards between 1903 and 1914 (in MEPO 6) and of habitual criminals between 1869 and 1940 (in PCOM 2 and MEPO 6). They contain a considerable amount of information, including photographs, aliases and distinguishing marks. This is how the black sheep of your family may have ended up!

Before 1829 Scotland had separate Customs and Excise boards. Records for men in these services are in T 43, with pay lists in T 45, although many records are at the NAS. After the unification of the services in 1829, the place to look is CUST 39, which includes pay lists and applications for pensions up to 1922. Coastguard service records are largely in ADM 175, which covers the period between about 1820 and 1923, although there are gaps.

Also useful are apprenticeship records. Between 1701 and 1804 apprenticeship indentures throughout Great Britain were subject to taxation. Indexes and records of those indentured and the masters to whom they were apprenticed are at the PRO. The SoG compiled the indexes and also holds a copy. Indexes for masters go up to 1762 and apprentices to 1774. However, there were many exemptions to the payment of the tax, particularly if a master was taking a child from an orphanage or off parish relief. In addition, there was wide-spread evasion.

Minor sources

These records may also be of interest:

- claims to Scottish peerages, 1822–39   HO 80

- Scottish peers' oath roll, 1837   C 214/21

- fiats for justices of burghs, 1823–1929;
  and counties, 1705–1973   C 234

- legal proceedings in Scotland after the 1745
  rebellion, including lists of rebels and prisoners   TS 20

- list of justices of the peace, 1708; entry book of
  justices, 1838–1975, and registers, 1879–1975   C 193

- list of passengers sailing from Greenwich to
  Scotland, 1667   E 157

- list of persons paying tax on carriages and silver
  plate, 1756–62   T 36

- muster rolls of the Scottish Army in England,
  1641   SP 41
- payments of superannuation and disablement
  allowances to teachers, 1903–28   PMG 53

- presentations to churches, 1724–1808   SP 56

SPECIALIST LIBRARIES

Society of Genealogists

The Society of Genealogists in London has Britain's finest genealogical library. It is free to members, and available to non-members for a fee. As well as the library, the Society also has a very good bookshop and runs a range of lectures and courses. It can be found near Barbican station at:

▼ **Society of Genealogists**
  14 Charterhouse Buildings
  Goswell Road
  London EC1M 7BA
  Telephone: 020 7251 8799
  Internet: http://www.sog.org.uk

The library is closed on Sundays and Mondays, on public holidays, and throughout the first full week of February.

Opening hours are:

Tuesday	10 a.m. to 6 p.m.
Wednesday	10 a.m. to 8 p.m.
Thursday	10 a.m. to 8 p.m.
Friday	10 a.m. to 6 p.m.
Saturday	10 a.m. to 6 p.m.

The library contains some 100,000 books, many of them unique, on a wide range of subjects. There are considerable holdings of microfilm and microfiche, as well as collections of people's research and family trees. The library's catalogue should be available on the Society's website (see p. 54) in the near future. Also, the Society's quarterly publication, *The Genealogist's Magazine*, contains lists of new additions to the library stock.

There is a very good introductory booklet called *Using the Library of the Society of Genealogists*, that explains the holdings and where they can be found. It is given to all new members and copies can also be purchased in the bookshop.

The SoG has considerable holdings of material relating to Scotland. There is a Scottish section, with the prefix SC, but in practice material is scattered round the library. The best guide to these holdings is Marjorie Moore's *Sources for Scottish Genealogy in the Library of the Society of Genealogists* (SoG, 1996). Unfortunately this book is now out of print, but it is well worth hunting down.

The records relevant to Scottish ancestry include:

- Indexes to Scottish civil registration between 1855 and 1920, and the certificates themselves for 1855.

- Microfilm and transcripts of many old parish registers (OPRs). The library computer catalogue and Moore, *Sources* indicate which ones the Society has and dates covered.

- Microfiche indexes to births or baptisms and marriages between 1553 and 1854 in all the old parochial registers for Scotland. These are arranged by county.

- Lists of Quaker baptisms, marriages and deaths between about 1656 and 1878.

- Scottish entries on the FamilySearch CD-ROMs and the *International Genealogical Index (IGI)* microfiche.

- Census indexes between 1841 and 1891.

- Monumental inscriptions for many cemeteries and churches throughout Scotland.

- Street and trade directories for many cities and towns. In addition, there may be local histories, guides and maps, particularly for the larger cities.

- Published lists of graduates from the universities of Aberdeen, Edinburgh, Glasgow and St Andrews.

- Published guides to the Scottish peerage and landed gentry.

- Indexes to newspapers held in Scottish libraries.

- Lists of irregular border marriages and marriages by special licence.

- Transcripts or other records relating to wills, including printed indexes of all the Scottish Commisariat Court Wills from 1514 to 1800 and for many places to 1830. There are also extracts of wills of Scottish people proved at the Prerogative Court of Canterbury and at courts in Australia and the United States.

- Various published accounts of emigration to North America, Australia and elsewhere.

The SoG library also has considerable holdings of periodicals. Of particular note is the run of the *Scottish Genealogist* from 1954, and the magazines and publications of Scottish family history societies. There are also many publications and journals of local history societies, and contemporary journals such as *Scots Magazine* (published 1740–1802), *Northern Notes and Queries,* and the *Gentleman's Magazine*, which contains information about the nobility and the landed gentry.

There are of course many Scottish entries in other books, particularly registers of professions, such as the *Army, Navy* and *Law Lists*, *Medical Registers*, and lists of Members of Parliament. The SoG also has standard reference books such as the *Dictionary of National Biography* and *Who was Who*. Other biographical sources particularly for Scotland include *The Scottish Nation: or the Surnames, Families, Literature, Honours and Biographical History of the People of Scotland* by William Anderson, published in three volumes between 1866 and 1877; an incomplete set of *A Biographical Dictionary of Eminent Scotsmen* by Robert Chambers, first published in 1835; and *Chambers' Scottish Biographical Dictionary*, edited by Rosemary Goring, published in 1992.

The SoG also holds published histories of a number of Scottish families as well as some records of clans, including a series of newspaper cuttings, arranged by clan, from the *Weekly Scotsman*. In addition there are large numbers of family trees (pedigrees) and collections of genealogical research papers (called Special Collections), which have been given to the Society over many years. The most important of these is probably the Macleod Collection, which was presented to the Society in 1949. It consists of case reports on families researched by Walter Macleod and his son John over a period of sixty years and transcripts from the OPRs. Both the Macleod Collection and the other collections and pedigrees are well indexed, so it is not difficult to check whether your family appears in this material. Another potentially useful source is the Document Collection: its boxes contain miscellaneous notes, documents and other material arranged in surname order. Additions to the Document Collection since 1992 are available only on microfilm.

Scottish Genealogy Society

The Society was founded in Edinburgh in 1953. Its aims are to promote research into Scottish family history and to undertake the collection, exchange and publication of material relating to genealogy.

The Society does not undertake research for members of the public, but offers a library and Family History Centre, which is open to non-members at a charge of £5 per day (price in 2000). The Centre is situated in the heart of the Old Town of Edinburgh, just off the Royal Mile, close to the Castle, the National Library of Scotland and the Edinburgh Central Library. The library is located on Victoria Terrace, which is above Victoria Street, in an 18th century building. Copying facilities are available for books, microfilm and microfiche.

▼ **Scottish Genealogy Society Library**
15 Victoria Terrace
Edinburgh EH1 2JL
Telephone: 0131 220 3677
Internet: http://www.scotsgenealogy.com

The library now contains thousands of books, journals and directories on various subjects, including:

- the peerage

- heraldry

- topography

- emigration

- school and university records

- military records

- private research

- individual families and clans

It also has:

- complete runs of journals from Scottish family history societies

- material relating to families in other countries, especially Ireland and the Commonwealth

- large holdings of microfiche, microfilm and CD-ROMs relating to records in Scotland and elsewhere in the United Kingdom, including a microfilm collection of about 70 per cent of the old parish registers of Scotland.

The Society has been actively engaged in transcribing gravestone inscriptions for many years. It has built up the largest collection of Scottish monumental inscriptions in the world. Published lists for many areas are on sale and photocopies of unpublished lists are available.

OTHER RESOURCES

The National Register of Archives (Scotland) – NRA(S) – acts as a clearing house of information on archives throughout Scotland. It can be very helpful if you are trying to find the records of a particular church or business. NRA(S) surveys of archives are available in the National Archives of Scotland's West Search Room, with many surveys searchable on computer. Written enquiries should be addressed to the Secretary, National Register of Archives (Scotland), HM General Register House, Edinburgh EH1 3YY, Scotland, or by email to nra@nas.gov.uk (telephone 0131 535 1405). Indexes to NRA(S) surveys are also available on the website of the Historical Manuscripts Commission in London (http://www.hmc.gov.uk).

As in England, there is a network of local archives and local studies libraries in Scotland. Because of the relative paucity of documents before 1800 and the greater role that the National Archives have traditionally played in the preservation of written records, the holdings of these bodies are likely to be less comprehensive than one might expect at an English county record office. One exception is the Mitchell Library in Glasgow, which has a superb collection relating to the city and the former region of Strathclyde. The address is: Mitchell Library, 210 North Street, Glasgow G3 7DN (telephone 0141 287 2913, website: http://www.glasgow.gov.uk).

A full list of Scottish archives and local studies libraries, together with a brief description of their holdings, is provided in M. Cox (ed.), *Exploring Scottish History* (Scottish Library Association, 1999).

GLOSSARY

Scottish records contain a number of terms and phrases that may be unfamiliar to readers, such as:

Executor	Person appointed to administer the moveable estate of the deceased
Heritable property	Property that cannot be moved – minerals in the ground and buildings
Inventory	List of the moveable property of the deceased
Kirk Sessions	Roughly equivalent to vestries or parish councils in England
Moveable property	Possessions that can be physically moved, furniture, animals, machinery and implements
Retours	Registers that recorded the transfer of heritable property. Special retours named the property, while general retours did not. Sometimes called services of heirs.
Sasines	Records noting the transfer of land
Services of heirs	See retours
Testament	Will
Testament-dative	Confirmation of the appointment of an executor if there is no will
Testament-testamentar	Confirmation of the appointment of an executor if there is a will

FURTHER READING

There are a number of books on Scottish genealogy, both general and detailed. Probably the most useful guide remains *Tracing Your Scottish Ancestors*, although it is now rather dated. *My Ain Folk* has a very good bibliography, while *Jock Tamson's Bairns* is a well-written introduction to why and how the most important genealogical records were created.

A. Bevan (ed.), *Tracing Your Ancestors in the Public Record Office*, 5th edn (PRO, 1999)

L.R. Burness, *A Scottish Historian's Glossary* (Association of Scottish Family History Societies, 1991)

M. Cox, *Exploring Scottish History,* 2nd edn (Scottish Library Association, 1999)

S. Fowler and W. Spencer, *Army Service Records for Family Historians* (PRO, 1998)

G.S. Holton and J. Winch, *My Ain Folk – An Easy Guide to Scottish Family History* (Tuckwell Press, 1997)

A. James, *Scottish Roots: A Step-By-Step Guide for Ancestor-Hunters* (Saltire Society, 1997)

R. Kershaw and M. Pearsall, *Immigrants and Aliens: A Guide to Sources on UK Immigration and Citizenship* (PRO, 2000)

M. Moore, *Sources for Scottish Genealogy in the Library of the Society of Genealogists* (Society of Genealogists, 1996)

P. Ruthven-Murray, *Scottish Census Indexes: A brief guide to the Availability of Census Indexes 1841–1871 and Where to Find Them.* (Association of Scottish Family History Societies, 1996)

C. Sinclair, *Jock Tamsin's Bairns: A History of the Records of the General Register Office for Scotland* (General Register Office for Scotland, 2000)

C. Sinclair, *Tracing Your Scottish Ancestors* (HMSO, 1990)

K. Smith, C. Watts and M. Watts, *Records of Merchant Shipping and Seamen* (PRO, 1998)

W. Spencer, *Air Force Records for Family Historians* (PRO, 2000)

S.M. Spiers, *Parishes, Registers & Registrars: A Complete List of Scottish Parish Registers* (Association of Scottish Family History Societies, 1997)

G. Thomas, *Records of the Royal Marines* (PRO, 1995)

C. Watts and M. Watts, *My Ancestor was a Merchant Seaman* (Society of Genealogists, 1986)

Recent and forthcoming publications from the PRO

Pocket Guides

Just published:

Tracing Catholic Ancestors, Michael Gandy (2001)
Tracing Nonconformist Ancestors, Michael Gandy (2001)
Tracing Irish Ancestors, Simon Fowler (2001)
Using Poor Law Records, Simon Fowler (2001)

Forthcoming:

Using Medal Records, William Spencer (2001)
Using Criminal Records, Simon Fowler (2001)
Using Education and Apprenticeship Records,
    Simon Fowler (2002)

Other forthcoming publications

The Genealogist's Internet, Peter Christian (2001)
Army Service Records of World War I (Expanded edition),
    William Spencer (2001)
Tracing the History of Your House, Nick Barratt (2001)
Railway Records, Cliff Edwards (2001)